Navigating Adolescence

CW00841118

Essential Life Skills Every

Boy Needs to Know

Disclaimer: The information provided in this book is for general informational purposes only.

The content of this book is not intended to be a substitute for professional advice, diagnosis, or treatment. Always seek the advice of your physician, mental health professional, or other qualified health provider with any questions you may have regarding a medical condition or mental health concerns.

The author and publisher disclaim any liability, loss, or risk incurred as a direct or indirect consequence of the use and application of any of the contents of this book. The reader is solely responsible for their actions and decisions based on the information provided herein. By reading this book, you agree to the terms of this disclaimer. If you do not agree with the terms of this disclaimer, you should not read or use the information provided in this book.

Acknowledgments

To my parents, thank you for instilling in me the values of perseverance, integrity, and compassion. Your unwavering love and encouragement have been the cornerstone of my growth. To my siblings thank you for your endless support and laughter along the way.

To my friends, both old and new, thank you for being my companions on this unpredictable journey. Your camaraderie, laughter, and shared experiences have brought immeasurable joy to my life – and if I can impart anything at all to the young readers it is to *value true friends*. Together, we have navigated the highs and lows, celebrated triumphs and provided comfort in times of misfortune.

To the readers of this book, your support and willingness to embark on this journey with me mean the world. It is my sincere hope that the insights and lessons shared within these pages empower you to embrace your own path, navigate life's challenges with resilience, and cultivate a meaningful and fulfilling existence.

Introduction

You're about to embark on an incredible adventure known as manhood.

This isn't just any journey; it's a personal odyssey filled with twists and turns, triumphs and trials, laughter, and tears.

Picture yourself standing at the edge of a boundless ocean. As you gaze out, all you see is an infinite expanse of deep blue water, stretching as far as the eye can see. Waves crash at your feet, their raw power and immense depth both thrilling and overwhelming.

This is adolescence - a time of immense potential and challenges that can feel as vast and unpredictable as the ocean itself.

> *"Life is a journey that must be traveled no matter how bad the roads and accommodations." - Oliver Goldsmith*

Your Journey to Manhood

This book 'Navigating Adolescence: Essential Life Skills Every Boy Needs to Know' will serve as your compass, guiding you safely through this ocean of adolescence, helping you to navigate the transition from boyhood to manhood with confidence and integrity.

Let's get something straight: growing up can be one heck of a roller-coaster ride! One moment you're riding high on cloud nine; the next minute life turns upside down like an inverted loop. It can feel exhilarating and terrifying all at once!

First, we'll understand adolescence itself - what's happening inside your body? Why are your emotions all over the place? We'll demystify puberty with simple science so that these changes won't catch you off guard anymore.

Next, we'll equip you with some essential life skills. Think of them as tools in your backpack, ready to be unleashed when needed. Financial literacy will help you build a solid foundation for your future. Cooking skills will ensure you never go hungry on this adventure. Personal hygiene will keep you healthy, and time management will help you navigate through the stormy seas of busy schedules.

Later, we'll explore building healthy relationships because let's face it—we need people around us—to share joys, divide sorrows or merely co-exist peacefully. But how do we communicate effectively? How do we understand consent? These are some questions that we will find the answers to in easy-to-understand language peppered with relatable examples.

Remember when Bilbo Baggins was reluctant to step out of his comfortable Hobbit hole fearing unexpected adventures? Yet once he did embark on that epic expedition in 'The Hobbit,' there was no looking back! Similarly stepping out of your childhood comfort zone might seem daunting initially but trust me—you're going to come out stronger, wiser & ready to conquer whatever life throws at you!

So, fasten your seatbelt! Your journey into manhood starts right here, right now! And always remember, every great journey begins with that first step.

"Growing into a man means embracing challenges, showing empathy, and making a positive impact in the world." Tristan Brody

Table of Contents

Chapter 1: Understanding Adolescence: The Transition from Boyhood to Manhood

Adolescence, that uncertain and exciting time when a boy begins his journey into manhood.

As you journey from boyhood to manhood, a lot is happening beneath the surface. This process is called puberty, and it's an important part of your life. It might seem confusing at times, but understanding what's going on can help make things easier. So let's dive in!

The Science Behind Puberty

"Puberty is characterized by hormonal, physical, and psychological transformation. The human brain undergoes significant changes between childhood and adulthood" (Anne-Lise Goddings, 2014).

According to science stuff, puberty usually hits boys somewhere between the ages of 9 and 14, but hey, everyone's body has its own timeline. You may be a little younger or a little older – and that's perfectly okay.

During puberty, your body goes through a series of changes; think of it as a massive upgrade to version 2.0! Your brain signals your body to produce hormones like testosterone that trigger some of these changes.

Coming to Terms with Physical Changes

You'll notice growth spurts where you suddenly shoot up in height and start developing muscles. Like, seriously, you might shoot up by 4 inches in a year!

Now here comes the interesting part - hair growth. You'll begin seeing hair growing in new places such as underarms, face, chest, and yes, even down there! This is because hair follicles are stimulated by testosterone during puberty.

In the fascinating journey of adolescence, boys experience a series of physical changes that mark the transition from boyhood to manhood.

One of the most natural and common occurrences during this time is the emergence of erections. These spontaneous and sometimes unexpected experiences are a normal part of growing up and signify the awakening of a young man's body.

It's important to understand that erections are a completely normal and healthy response to various stimuli, such as physical touch, visual stimulation, thoughts and hormones. While they may feel new and unfamiliar, embracing this change with knowledge and understanding will empower boys to navigate this phase of their lives with confidence and self-assurance.

And let's not forget your voice change; one day you're sounding like a young squeaky Justin Bieber and the next day your voice is as deep as Barry White! That's because your voice box or larynx grows larger during this phase.

And lastly, if you are like most teens, acne may become a common sight on your face, chest, and even back due to increased oil production in the skin glands. Don't worry though; this usually clears up after puberty.

Behind all these changes is a hormone called testosterone, produced by your testes. This hormone is like the boss of puberty, responsible for developing your masculine traits and even affecting your moods and energy levels. It's like having the Incredible Hulk's superpower running through your veins!

Puberty isn't just about the physical stuff, though. Your brain is going through some serious remodeling too. Scientists say your brain is getting an upgrade, and it's affecting how you think and behave. So don't be surprised if you feel like you're in a constant state of "Who am I?" during this time. It's all part of the journey!

Mental and Emotional Changes in Adolescence

The physical changes are easy to see, but don't forget about the crazy mental and emotional transformations happening inside too!

Get ready for mood swings that seem to come out of nowhere. One moment you're laughing with your crew, and the next, you're feeling like the world is against you. It can be confusing, but hey, it's just part of the growing-up package deal.

Oh, and get ready to be overly sensitive! Things that used to roll off your back, like your mom telling you to clean your room, might hit you like a ton of bricks now. Emotions are cranked up to eleven, my friend. The highs are higher, the lows are lower, and everything in between feels like a roller coaster drop.

"Hormone reactivity to stressors and hormones that rapidly change at puberty are hypothesized to influence moods, which may, in turn, affect parent-child relationship quality." (Marceau, 2012)

Now, let's talk about relationships. Friendships take on a whole new level of awesome, and you might even start feeling the butterflies of romance for the first time. It's exciting, but...it can get pretty complicated too. We'll go into more depth about relationships a bit later in the book.

You'll feel this strong urge to break free from your parents' grip and carve out your own path. Independence is calling! It's all part of figuring out who you are as an individual. Just remember to keep the communication lines open with your loved ones, even as you spread your wings.

Last but not least, let's talk about self-consciousness. Suddenly, you're hyper-aware of your appearance, and you might worry about what others think of you. It's normal to feel a bit anxious or insecure about these things. Just remember, you're awesome just the way you are.

Common Misconception

You might hear advice suggesting suppressing emotions because 'real men don't cry'. Let us debunk this myth right away! Expressing emotions doesn't make anyone less masculine rather it shows strength in being your authentic self.

Real Life Story: Meet Kevin

Let's introduce you to Kevin, a typical 16-year-old guy. One moment, he was hanging out with friends, playing video games, and obsessing over superheroes. Then suddenly he woke up each morning to a brand-new surprise—acne popping up like unwanted guests, a voice cracking like a broken stereo and clothes that seemed to shrink overnight. It was as if his body had signed him up for a wild ride without a safety net.

One freezing winter night, Kevin gazed at his reflection in the mirror. The face staring back seemed different, not quite the boyish image he once had in his mind. His shoulders were broadening, and his hair sprouted in unexpected places. Changes were happening, and they felt strange yet inevitable.

But his mind wasn't spared from the turmoil either. Emotions raged like they were on a caffeine-fueled rampage—elation one minute, anger the next, followed by a bout of unexplained sadness. It felt like he was riding an unpredictable wave, and man, was it wild!

Kevin found comfort in knowing that he wasn't alone in this whirlwind. This chaotic journey is a universal rite of passage that teenagers across all cultures and throughout history have experienced.

He channeled his swirling emotions into creative outlets. He picked up his dad's dusty old guitar, strumming away to release what his words couldn't express. And when inspiration struck, he scribbled down verses that painted his feelings in vivid colors.

Kevin also took better care of his changing body. He resisted the tempting call of junk food and chose healthier options. Even when laziness whispered sweet nothings, he laced up his shoes and hit the football field for practice and fresh air.

But most importantly, Kevin learned to be kinder to himself during this chaotic period. He realized that some days would be tougher than others, and that's okay. Growing up isn't an overnight transformation—it's a gradual process of self-discovery and finding our place in the world.

*Ah-ha Moment: Understanding why these changes occur helps us realize they're a normal part of growing up and **not something wrong with us individually**. Knowing how hormones influence our bodies gives us power over our reactions instead of feeling controlled by them.*

Key Takeaways

- Puberty triggers physical changes transforming boys into men.

- Emotional fluctuations are common due to brain development.

- Suppressing feelings isn't healthy or beneficial.

- Understand that experiencing mood swings is normal during adolescence.

- Reach out for help if needed; there's no shame in seeking guidance.

- Open communication about ongoing bodily alterations can reduce confusion or anxiety associated with them.

Chapter 2: Developing Essential Life Skills

Welcome to a chapter packed with essential life skills that will empower you my extraordinary friend to navigate the complexities of adulthood with grace and confidence.

In this chapter, we'll embark on a transformative journey that covers four crucial pillars: financial literacy, cooking, personal hygiene, and time management.

These skills are the cornerstones of a well-rounded and thriving life. We'll dive into the captivating world of financial literacy, equipping you with the knowledge and tools to make smart money decisions.

We'll also explore the delicious realm of cooking, as you unlock the secrets to basic recipes and food safety, ensuring that you can nourish yourself and impress others with your culinary prowess.

Furthermore, we'll delve into the importance of personal hygiene and grooming, providing you with the know-how to take care of your body and present your best self to the world.

Lastly, we'll tackle time management skills, teaching you the art of balancing schoolwork, hobbies, and personal time to maximize productivity and well-being. So buckle up, because this chapter is your all-in-one guide to mastering essential life skills and setting the stage for a future filled with success, health, and happiness. Let's dive in!

Financial Literacy for Teens: Saving, Spending, and Earning Money

As you embark on the journey of financial independence, a wave of excitement and maybe a hint of nervousness might wash over you. Suddenly, you have the power to earn your own hard-earned cash, spend it as you please, and save up for epic future goals.

But hold up, with this newfound freedom comes responsibility. But don't fret! This chapter is here to be your trusty guide, showing you the ropes of managing your finances like a boss.

Ever wonder why some people always seem to have stacks of cash while others are constantly scraping by? Well, it's all about financial literacy, my friends. It's the secret sauce to understanding how money works in the real world.

And guess what? Money management is less about crunching numbers and more about having *the right mindset*. It's about grasping concepts like saving up, spending wisely, and earning that moolah.

So, let's dive right in and unlock the core of financial literacy.

"By developing essential life skills, a boy equips himself with the tools to navigate the challenges and seize the opportunities that lie ahead." Bradley Turner

Picture this: three simple strategies that will set you on the path to financial success.

First Up, Saving Regularly...

Now, I know what you're thinking. Saving is probably only for grown-ups who have bills to pay and retirement plans to think about. Well, think again!

Even for young guns like you, saving is the key to unlocking the treasures of life. The sooner you start, the better off you will be in the long run.

Whether it's that shiny new smartphone or an epic trip abroad after graduation, these dreams require some serious cash. Start small if you need to but make it a habit to tuck away a portion of your earnings into your savings account. Your future self will thank you.

A basic formula to use is 5% of what you earn goes into a bank account that you don't touch. So, for every $10 you earn – you put 50 cents away in a bank account. Does that sound achievable? Sure does, and you'll be surprised just how quickly that 5% savings starts to add up. If you find yourself saving 5% easily – challenge yourself to save 10%.

Case studies have shown young people who start working part-time jobs during high school tend to develop better work ethics and understand the value of hard-earned cash (Jeylan T. Mortimer, 2010).

Next on Our Financial Adventure is Spending...

Let me tell you, it's the part where things can get seriously thrilling—or seriously dicey.

Impulse buys, my friends, are the sly villains that can drain your funds faster than you can say, "I'm broke."

But fear not! Before you swipe that card or hit that "buy now" button, take a step back and ask yourself—is this purchase worth it? Does it bring true value to your life? By thoughtfully considering your purchases, you can dodge the traps of overspending and come out on top.

Hold onto your hats because here's a mind-blowing fact: _teens who learn how to manage their expenses wisely are more likely to rock their financial stability later in life._

Real-Life Example: Rachel and Mark

Let's look at Rachel and Mark for a moment. Rachel rarely saved anything and splurged on designer sneakers without considering her budget, while Mark was a strategic mastermind, carefully planning his purchases within his monthly allowance and even setting aside some emergency funds.

Guess who ended up with extra cash in their pocket?

You got it—Mark. Rachel, on the other hand, found herself always scrambling before payday and never having any money saved.

The lesson here is loud and clear, **actions speak louder than words** when it comes to being a financial superstar.

Lastly, Let's Look at Earning Money...

It's not just about the dollars and cents, my friends. It's about understanding the value of your blood, sweat, and tears. Trust me, it'll change the way you spend.

Think of it as a badge of honor, a symbol of your hustle and determination. When you work those part-time jobs during high school, you're not only raking in some extra dough but also developing a killer work ethic.

That's the secret sauce to appreciating the value of your hard-earned cash. The National Bureau of Economic Research knows what's up.

Ready for some cool tips and tricks? Buckle up because here they come:

1. Pay **yourself** first by saving before you even think about spending. Put 5% of your wages away in a bank account that you use for your future – trust me, you'll thank yourself in 10 years.

2. Ask yourself if it's a ***need*** or just a ***want*** before making that purchase.

3. Keep your eyes peeled for ***student*** and ***sale discounts***. Trust me, they're golden. But make sure you need it, don't just buy it because it's on sale! *It's all about balance and you are allowed to indulge every once in a while – as long as you have saved for it!*

Oh, and here's an eye-opener—according to the Charles Schwab Foundation's 'Teens & Money Survey, 2006', nearly two-thirds of teens confessed they know little about handling money, even though they consider themselves savvy spenders.

It just goes to show that there's often a gap between what we think we know and what we actually understand when it comes to finance.

Keep that fire for knowledge burning bright. Read articles and books about personal finance to expand your understanding. Remember, the learning never stops on your journey to mastering the art of managing money like a pro.

So, my young financial warriors, go forth with your newfound knowledge and conquer the world of finance. You've got this!

A Beginner's Guide to Cooking: Basic Recipes and Food Safety

Get ready to unleash your inner chef and buckle up for a thrilling adventure into the magical realm of basic recipes and food safety.

Picture this: you throw on your stylish apron like a superhero cape, armed with spatulas and mixing bowls, ready to conquer the kitchen. But before we jump into culinary action, let's talk about our secret weapon—food safety!

Imagine your kitchen as a battleground and harmful bacteria are the sneaky enemies lurking in your food. But fear not, because we've got a foolproof plan to defeat them!

First, it's all about keeping things clean. Wash your hands, utensils, and surfaces like a boss.

Second, let's not have any food cross-contamination parties. Keep raw meat away from other foods and let them dance solo.

Third, the power of heat is your ally. Cook your food at the right temperatures to send those bacteria running. And lastly, don't forget to chill out! Promptly refrigerate your leftovers to prevent any uninvited guests from having a feast.

Now that we're armed with our basic food safety armor, it's time for some culinary wizardry! The first few times you do this, I recommend having your mom or dad watch over you until you are confident.

Let's start with a classic breakfast favorite—scrambled eggs.

Scrambled Eggs

These little fluffy clouds of protein-packed goodness are a surefire way to start your day with a bang.

Here's how you make them:

1. Crack two eggs into a bowl.

2. Add a splash of milk and a pinch of salt and pepper.

3. Whisk until yolks and whites blend into sunshine yellow.

4. Heat a knob of butter over medium heat in a non-stick pan until it melts.

5. Pour egg mixture and stir gently (like you'd treat a puppy) until soft curds form.

Voila! Your scrambled eggs are ready. Serve up your soft delicious eggs on some toast, or better yet, with a side of bacon.

But wait, there's more! Get ready for a taste of Italy with spaghetti Aglio e Olio.

Spaghetti Aglio e Olio

Don't let the fancy name fool you; it's as easy as saying ABC.

Ingredients

- 1 pound uncooked spaghetti

- ½ cup olive oil

- 6 cloves garlic, thinly sliced (or just use a couple of teaspoons of minced garlic from a jar!)

- ¼ teaspoon red pepper flakes to taste

- salt and freshly ground black pepper to taste

- ¼ cup chopped fresh Italian parsley

- 1 cup finely grated Parmigiano-Reggiano cheese

Follow these steps:

1. Bring a large pot of lightly salted water to a boil. Cook spaghetti in the boiling water, stirring occasionally until cooked through but firm to the bite (al dente), about 10 to 12 minutes. Drain and transfer to a pasta bowl.

2. In another pan, combine olive oil and garlic in a cold skillet. Heat until a medium-low when olive oil begins to bubble. Place the garlic in the pan and cook and stir until garlic is golden brown, about 5 minutes. Remove from heat.

3. Stir red pepper flakes, salt, and black pepper into pasta. Pour in hot olive oil and garlic, and sprinkle on Italian parsley and half of the Parmigiano-Reggiano cheese; toss it all together with some tongs until combined.

4. Serve pasta topped with the remaining Parmigiano-Reggiano cheese.

Mamma Mia! You've just unlocked level one of Italian cuisine!

Now, let's address the elephant in the kitchen—mistakes. They happen to the best of us, and that's okay!

If your scrambled eggs turn out rubbery or your pasta feels a bit mushy, don't panic. Every mistake is a golden opportunity to learn and improve your skills. As the legendary chef Julia Child once said, "The only real stumbling block is the fear of failure."

Embrace those mishaps, laugh them off, and keep experimenting. And remember, even if things go completely south, there's always the trusty 'emergency pizza delivery' to save the day!

One last word my brave young chefs, always prioritize food safety in your culinary adventures. Start simple to build your confidence, and never be afraid to make mistakes. So put on that apron, embrace the sizzle of the stove (supervised), and let your culinary creativity shine. Happy cooking!

Personal Hygiene and Grooming: Taking Care of Your Body

Now, I know what you might be thinking: "I've been taking showers since forever, what's the big deal?"

Well, my friend, as your body undergoes changes in this transition to adulthood, your grooming routine needs a little upgrade too.

Did you know that our bodies have not one, but two types of sweat glands? We've got the eccrine glands that secrete water-based sweat all over our bodies, and then there are the apocrine glands, mainly found in places like our underarms, that secrete a thicker substance that can cause an odor when bacteria break it down. Pretty fascinating, right?

But fret not! Understanding these nifty details about how our bodies work will help us navigate the realm of personal hygiene like true champions. So, stick with me through this, and I promise you'll come out feeling confident and ready to tackle your daily grooming routine like a pro.

Now, let's dive deeper into the world of personal hygiene. The first stop on our grooming adventure is bathing. When it comes to showering or bathing frequency, there isn't a one-size-fits-all answer.

Some folks might benefit from a daily shower to remove excess oils and dirt, while others might find that every other day works best for their unique skin type. If you play lots of sports, you may find you need two showers a day, and that's totally okay too.

Remember those apocrine glands we chatted about earlier? Well, during puberty, they become active, which can lead to increased body odor. That's where deodorant becomes your trusty sidekick in the battle against unpleasant smells. A good deodorant is antibacterial and helps prevent odors. As you start to hit adolescence make it a part of your daily routine, your friends will thank you too.

Brushing your teeth twice a day is a non-negotiable habit, but let's take it up a notch. Consider flossing regularly to remove plaque buildup between your pearly whites, where your toothbrush can't reach. It's the secret weapon to maintaining a killer smile.

The American Dental Association (ADA) found that brushing twice a day reduces the risk of cavities by a whopping 50% compared to once-a-day brushers.

As we've talked about., a solid hygiene routine includes regular baths or showers using mild soap suitable for your skin type, applying deodorant daily to combat body odor, and keeping your oral health in check through brushing and flossing.

But here's the cherry on top. Good personal hygiene goes beyond just keeping bad odors at bay. It plays a crucial role in preventing illnesses caused by harmful bacteria or viruses, like the flu or common cold, which thrive in dirty environments.

Did you know that simple handwashing alone can prevent 1 in 5 respiratory infections, including pneumonia? It's true! Taking steps towards better hygiene not only enhances social acceptance but also offers significant health benefits.

Good personal hygiene isn't just about fitting into society's norms—it's about safeguarding your physical health and reducing the risk of illnesses caused by pesky pathogens.

Now, let's zoom out and take a broader look at cleanliness. It's not just about our bodies; it includes the spaces around us too! Regularly clean high-touch surfaces like phone screens and computer keyboards and change your bed linen weekly.

Remember, maintaining cleanliness extends beyond ourselves; it includes our surroundings. By keeping our spaces tidy and germ-free, we enhance our overall well-being.

According to reports from the CDC, approximately 80% of diseases are transmitted through touching contaminated objects. That's why cleanliness in our surroundings is vital to reduce the risks of disease transmission. So, let's keep our spaces squeaky clean!

Now, let's get hands-on with some tips for better body care:

1. Choose skin products suitable for your specific skin type or concerns. If you have pimples like I did, consider using acne-fighting products recommended by a dermatologist.

2. Avoid harsh soaps that strip away your skin's natural oils.

3. Pay attention to cleaning behind your ears, where oil build-up is often overlooked. Focus on areas prone to sweat, like your underarms, groin, and feet. Washing away dirt, sweat, and bacteria helps keep your body clean and fresh.

4. Use lukewarm water instead of hot water to preserve your skin's natural moisture barrier.

With these steps incorporated into your daily routine, managing personal hygiene will soon become second nature. And trust me, my friend, confidence will be your companion as you navigate the intriguing journey called adulthood. So embrace the world of personal hygiene with gusto and let your inner hygiene guru shine!

Time Management: Juggling Schoolwork, Hobbies, and Personal Time

Have you ever felt like a circus performer, juggling schoolwork, hobbies, and personal time? Trust me, you're not alone in this daring act. It's a common struggle for most teenagers, but fear not!

Just like the skillful juggler who practices tirelessly to perfect his act, you too can conquer the art of balance with a few clever tricks up your sleeve.

Let's dive into the science behind time management because it's not just about cramming more activities into your day. It's about managing your energy effectively.

According to the research wizards Tony Schwartz and Jim Loehr in "The Power of Full Engagement," our energy operates in cycles.

We can focus intensely for around **90 minutes** before needing a break. So, keep this in mind while scheduling your tasks, and remember to take short breaks between intense study sessions or hobby classes to recharge your superpowers.

But wait, there's a secret technique!

Let's imagine your day as a giant empty jug, waiting to be filled with all the vibrant marbles of schoolwork, hobbies, and personal time. Each of these marbles has its own color—schoolwork is fiery red, hobbies are cool blue, and personal time is refreshing green. Your mission is to fit all these marbles into the jug without it overflowing—that's the true art of work-life balance!

Now, picture pouring sand, representing unimportant tasks, into the jug first. What happens? **There's barely any space left for the important marbles**, right?

Now, let's flip the script. Imagine placing big rocks, symbolizing your priorities, into the jug first. And then, as if by magic, you can pour the sand around the rocks, and everything fits perfectly!

This metaphor teaches us the importance of *prioritizing tasks effectively to create that ideal balance*.

*Ah-ha Moment: Remember, prioritization is the key to mastering time management—always tackle the **important** tasks (big rocks) before dealing with the less critical ones (sand).*

To bring this balance to life, consider creating a schedule or using productivity apps on your smartphone. Plan out each day, assigning specific blocks of time for studying, practicing your hobbies, and enjoying some well-deserved relaxation. By doing so, you ensure that each aspect of your life receives equal attention without overlapping or neglecting any of them.

> *"The bad news is time flies. The good news is you're the pilot." - Michael Altshuler*

These wise words remind us that understanding how much time we have isn't enough; what truly matters is how we *choose to use it.*

Now, let's tackle the sneaky termites known as distractions. They come in all shapes and forms, from tempting social media notifications to friends inviting you out when you need to study.

But fear not, my friend, for you possess the secret weapon against distractions—discipline! Make a pact with yourself: no Instagram or Snap Chat until **after** homework, or no video gaming until after you've rocked your basketball practice! Stay true to your word and watch those distractions melt away.

Ah-ha Moment: Level up your focus and crush your study sessions by turning off your app notifications like a boss!

And remember, consistency is your trusty sidekick on this journey.

If things still seem overwhelming despite your best efforts, take a deep breath, and remember, it's okay to ask for help. Reach out to your parents or teachers for advice on how to best manage your workload. They're there to support you on this adventure.

Remember, mastering the balancing act between schoolwork, hobbies, and personal time doesn't happen overnight. It's a continuous effort that will serve you well beyond your high school years, making your life both enjoyable and productive. So, my friend, embrace the challenge, sharpen your time-management skills, and get ready to conquer the world one perfectly balanced day at a time!

Key Takeaways

- Earning money responsibly can develop a work ethic and teach the value of hard-earned cash.

- Prioritizing needs over wants helps keep your finances under control and prevents overspending.

- Mastering basic cooking skills empowers you to create delicious and nutritious meals for yourself and others.

- Following recipes and practicing proper food safety measures, ensures safe and hygienic cooking.

- Maintaining good personal hygiene, such as regular bathing and brushing teeth, promotes physical health and prevents illnesses.

- Using deodorant or antiperspirant daily helps control body odor and keeps you feeling fresh throughout the day.

- Prioritizing tasks based on importance and deadlines helps you allocate your time wisely and accomplish your goals.

Chapter 3: Building Healthy Relationships

When you think about relationships, what comes to mind? Love, shared interests, or maybe even communication? Surprisingly, **communication** often gets overlooked, yet it's the key to expressing ourselves and connecting with others on a deeper level.

In my years of experience working with relationships, I've realized just how important effective communication is. It not only strengthens bonds but also prevents misunderstandings and conflicts.

The exciting part? Great communicators aren't born; they're made through practice! And you have the power to become one too!

Communicating Effectively with Peers, Family, and Teachers

Now, let's dive into the heart of the matter - mastering effective communication. Everyone has a unique communication style that develops over time due to various factors like family upbringing or cultural background.

Why is effective communication so crucial in building healthy relationships? Well, it fosters understanding by bridging gaps in perception and interpretation. It helps prevent resentment or disappointment by clarifying expectations.

Imagine playing a game of basketball or football without any form of communication with your team members - chaotic, right? Relationships, whether family or friendships, work the same way. Without a proper channel for expressing emotions and ideas, misunderstandings crop up, leading to discord.

"Communication leads to community — that is, understanding, intimacy, and mutual valuing." - Rollo May

This quote perfectly captures the essence of effective communication - bringing people together through shared understanding and appreciation.

Successful communicators consistently employ techniques like **active listening, empathy, and assertiveness**. By incorporating these strategies into your daily interactions, you'll notice improvements not only in personal relationships but also in academic settings where clear and concise exchanges are paramount.

Active Listening

Active listening is like turning up the volume on your communication skills. It's not just about hearing words; it's about truly tuning in and *giving your full attention* to the person speaking. When you actively listen, you engage with the speaker, making eye contact and using body language to show that you're genuinely interested.

You *resist the urge to interrupt* or jump in with your own thoughts, allowing them to express themselves fully. By mastering the art of active listening, you'll become a pro at understanding others, building stronger connections, and becoming a respected communicator. So, turn up that listening dial and let the magic happen!

A study published in "The International Journal of listening" found that teenagers who practiced active listening significantly improved their relationships with peers compared to those who didn't (Harry Weger, 2014).

Body Language

Nonverbal cues play a significant role in effective communication.

Body language is like a secret language we all speak, without even realizing it. It's the way we communicate our thoughts and emotions through our gestures, facial expressions, and posture.

Just think about how a confident stance and a friendly smile can make you instantly approachable, or how crossing your arms and avoiding eye contact can create a barrier between you and others.

Being aware of your own body language and paying attention to others' cues can give you valuable insights into their feelings and intentions. So, straighten those shoulders, keep your head up, and let your body speak volumes in every interaction.

Did you know that approximately **93%** of our overall message comes across nonverbally?

Only 7% of meaning is communicated through spoken word, 38% through tone of voice and the other 55% is made up from body language - facial expressions playing a crucial part when communicating with others (Mehrabian A., 1971).

Assert Yourself Respectfully

Asserting yourself respectfully is all about finding the balance between expressing your thoughts and feelings while still respecting the perspectives of others.

It starts with using "I" statements to clearly communicate your needs and concerns *without* placing blame on others.

Listen actively to the other person's point of view and show empathy toward their feelings. Maintain a calm and confident demeanor, using a firm but polite tone of voice. Remember, assertiveness is about standing up for yourself *without stepping on others.*

By practicing respectful assertiveness, you can effectively communicate your boundaries, opinions, and desires while maintaining positive relationships with those around you.

These steps may seem challenging at first, but remember, Rome wasn't built in a day, and your mastery of communication won't happen overnight.

With patience and persistence, you'll see remarkable improvements in your interpersonal connections, making the journey worthwhile in the end!

Understanding Consent and Respecting Personal Boundaries

It's important to note that consent goes beyond just sexual interactions. It applies to all aspects of life, including friendships, personal boundaries, and even sharing personal information.

Respecting someone's consent means respecting their autonomy and recognizing that they have the right to control what happens to their own body and personal information, including social media photos or things shared in private chat.

Let's start by defining consent. In its simplest form, consent is permission for something to happen or agreement to do something. However, when it comes to personal interactions that range from everyday conversations to intimate relationships, this definition expands significantly.

Real-Life Story: Taylor Swift

Remember that time back in 2017 when Taylor Swift took a stand in court?

Yeah, she wasn't gonna let anyone get away with crossing her boundaries. Swift didn't hold back when she described how violated and outraged, she felt after being 'groped' by a radio host without any consent. Groping is defined by the Oxford dictionary as 'to fondle (someone) for sexual pleasure roughly or clumsily, or without the person's consent.'

This whole incident is a perfect example of why consent is so important. Whether it's physical or emotional, we all have our limits and we must respect other people's boundaries.

Her bravery inspired people around the world who have gone through similar experiences. We need more stories like Taylor Swift's court case. We need to make consent conversations a normal part of our lives instead of hiding from them.

Let's create an environment where everyone feels safe and respected. Where 'no' means 'no' and it's okay to assert our own boundaries without fear.

Remember, consent is about recognizing each other's rights and boundaries. It's about **treating each other as humans** with individual autonomy. Whether it's at school, at home, or anywhere else, understanding consent is key to building respect between people.

So, as you go about your relationships - personal or professional - let Taylor Swift's courage inspire you. Let her remind you that respecting someone's boundaries is a reflection of **your** character. Be the kind of person who understands and respects consent.

Dealing with Peer Pressure

You're at a crossroads, my friend, where peer pressure seems to be lurking around every corner. It's a normal part of being a teenager, but don't worry, we've all been there.

And let me tell you, your friends' opinions can feel pretty influential. Now, peer pressure isn't all bad. It can push you to do great things like study harder or join a sports team. The tricky part is when it leads you down a risky path or makes you do things that go *against your values.*

So, how do you deal with it? It's all about knowing yourself and standing your ground.

Ah-ha Moment: here's the deal...you are way more important than any group or clique. You have your own identity, and that's something to be proud of!

A study showed that teenagers who give in to negative peer pressure tend to have lower self-esteem, while those who *stay true to themselves* have higher self-esteem, particularly for boys (M. Bámaca, A. Umaña-Taylor, 2006).

Real-Life Story: Meet John and Sam

Let me tell you a story about John. He was on the basketball team, but he started hanging out with a group that was all about skipping classes and partying hard.

Before he knew it, he was missing practices and going to wild parties fueled by alcohol.

Deep down, he wasn't comfortable with it, but he wanted to fit in, so he kept partying and staying out late. Before long, his grades had dropped, and the coach told him to lift his game, or he would be cut from the team.

Now, let's take a different path with Sam. He was a geeky introvert who loved comics and coding. His classmates made fun of him for it, but he refused to change himself just to fit in.

And you know what? Years later, he created an app based on one of his favorite comic characters, and it became a huge success!

It's important to know that negative peer pressure can have serious consequences. A report from the National Institute on Drug Abuse shows that around 55% of teens have tried drugs simply because their friends were doing it. That's a scary statistic, my friend.

Now, let's imagine a few scenarios:

Scenario A: Your friends invite you to smoke after school. Action Step: Politely decline and suggest doing something else, like catching a movie. If they say no, you can politely decline to join them and say you are heading to the movies anyway.

Scenario B: Everyone's making fun of thrift store finds while they wear designer clothes. Action Step: Stand tall and proudly embrace your unique and affordable fashion choices. Who cares what they think?

Scenario C: Your buddies want to ditch class to hang out. Action Step: Express your desire to maintain good academic performance and suggest meeting up after school instead.

I won't lie, it can be tough to stand up to peer pressure, but every small act of resistance strengthens your integrity and builds resilience for future challenges.

Stay strong and committed to finding yourself amid all the chaos that comes with adolescence. You've got this!

Navigating the World of Dating

Welcome to the exhilarating world of dating!

Get ready to set sail on a thrilling adventure, where each step you take brings you closer to understanding the mysteries of teenage romance. This guide is your trusty companion, filled with wisdom and advice to help you navigate the choppy waters and overcome the challenges that come with dating.

Don't be surprised if your early dating experiences feel like an obstacle course rather than a smooth sailing journey. But fear not! These experiences are an opportunity for personal growth and developing important life skills that will benefit you not only in relationships but also in your future professional endeavors.

Now, let's dive deep into the heart of the matter - navigating the world of teenage dating. Each phase of dating comes with its own set of unique challenges and rewards, and it's essential to understand the basics.

Dating is about getting to know someone better and enjoying each other's company. It can start with friendship or a romantic feeling with butterflies in your stomach - both are perfectly okay!

Drawing from my years of experience, I've gathered a series of tips that will make your journey smoother:

These simple foundations lay the groundwork for successful relationships. **Stay true to yourself** and master the art of **open communication** early on.

Real-Life Example: Meet Jake and Lucas

Meet Jake, a 16-year-old with a passion for music and art. He's never been one to conform to societal norms or change who he is just to impress someone. When it comes to dating, Jake knows that staying true to his hobbies and interests is the key to finding a genuine connection.

In the world of dating, it's easy to feel pressured to conform to the interests of your potential partner, especially if they seem vastly different from your own. But not Jake. He understands that the right person will appreciate him for who he truly is, quirks and all.

So, when Jake goes on a date, he confidently shares his love for music and art. He doesn't try to pretend he's into something he's not or hide his passions to please someone else.

Instead, he engages his date in conversations about his favorite bands, the latest art exhibit he visited, or the guitar he's learning to play.

Jake's authenticity is magnetic. His genuine enthusiasm for his hobbies is contagious, and it often sparks interesting conversations with his dates. Even if they don't share the same interests, they can't help but admire Jake's passion and dedication.

Sometimes, dating can feel like walking a tightrope between being yourself and trying to impress the other person. But Jake knows that compromising his authenticity to fit someone else's mold is a recipe for a short-lived connection. Instead, he values the importance of finding common ground without sacrificing who he is.

When Jake meets someone who shares his love for music or art, it's like finding a treasure trove of shared experiences. They can attend concerts together, explore art galleries hand in hand, and even play music together. But even if his date's interests differ, Jake approaches it with an open mind and curiosity, eager to learn about their passions.

By staying true to himself and being open-minded about his date's interests, Jake fosters a deeper level of connection with others. He realizes that dating is not about finding someone exactly like him, but rather someone who appreciates and respects his uniqueness.

And then there's Lucas, Meet Lucas, who understands the power of open communication in building strong relationships. From a young age, Lucas realized that holding back his thoughts and feelings only created barriers between him and others. So, he made a conscious effort to break down those barriers by being honest and transparent about what he thinks and feels.

In his friendships and dating, Lucas doesn't shy away from expressing his true emotions. If he's happy, he lets his friends know, and if he's upset, he doesn't hide it. This open and authentic communication creates a sense of trust and vulnerability that strengthens his friendships, allowing him and his friends to support each other through the highs and lows of life.

When it comes to dating, Lucas's approach to open communication is a game-changer. He doesn't play games or leave others guessing about how he feels. Instead, he openly expresses his interest in someone or communicates his boundaries and expectations. This upfront honesty allows both him and his potential partner to understand each other better and fosters a deeper level of trust and connection.

Through mastering the art of open communication, Lucas has developed healthier and more fulfilling relationships. He knows that being true to himself and expressing his thoughts and feelings openly lays the foundation for meaningful connections with others.

Analyzing these examples reveals valuable insights into what works and what doesn't in teenage dating. The common denominator? **Respectful communication** combined with **genuine self-expression** forms the bedrock of healthy relationships at any age.

Ah-ha Moment: Respect cannot be emphasized enough! Treating others with kindness and respect not only applies to love but also to all aspects of life.

Now, let's talk about actionable steps to become skilled navigators in the complex realm of teen dating!

Action Steps:

1. **Understand Your Feelings** - Pay attention to your emotions, such as happiness, anxiety, or jealousy, and acknowledge them.

2. **Express Yourself Clearly** - Use "I" statements to communicate your feelings instead of blaming or criticizing.

3. **Practice Active Listening** - Make sure she feels heard by offering feedback and asking clarifying questions.

4. **Stay True to Yourself** - Never compromise your core values or beliefs just to impress someone else!

5. **Exercise Patience** - Remember, good things take time. Don't rush into anything prematurely!

6. **Keep Learning and Growing** - Mistakes happen to everyone; use them as opportunities for growth rather than dwelling on them negatively.

Dating isn't easy, my friend, but then again, neither is sailing uncharted waters! Equipped with these valuable tools, you're well-prepared to navigate the exciting world of dating. Set sail with confidence and enjoy the journey ahead. Happy navigating!

Key Takeaways

- Active listening involves focusing entirely on the speaker instead of formulating responses while they're still talking.

- Clearly express your needs and feelings without disrespecting others' perspectives, using "I" statements instead of "you."

- Learn how to say no politely. We also spoke about how to be assertive in the pages on communication.

- Be respectful when dating - treat others the way you want to be treated.

- Be genuine: Authenticity is incredibly attractive.

- Good communication fosters healthy relationships. Listen attentively to her/him and express yourself clearly and honestly. Show empathy and understanding towards her/his feelings.

Chapter 4: Cultivating Emotional Intelligence

Emotional intelligence is the secret superpower that sets apart those who soar in life from those who stumble along the way.

It's all about understanding and managing your emotions, as well as recognizing and empathizing with the emotions of others. Picture it like a mental toolkit that helps you navigate the ups and downs of teenage life with grace and resilience.

Why does emotional intelligence matter? Well, imagine you're on a roller coaster ride of emotions - from the exhilaration of success to the frustration of failure. With emotional intelligence, you gain the power to understand and control those emotions, making better decisions and building stronger relationships.

It's like having a compass that guides you through stormy seas, helping you stay calm, make thoughtful choices, and connect with others on a deeper level. So, my friend, buckle up and get ready to harness your emotional intelligence to become the superhero of your own life!

Identifying and Expressing Emotions Healthily

Growing up as boys, we're often told to be tough and hide our emotions, as if it's a sign of weakness to express how we truly feel.

But let me tell you something my friend: embracing your emotions and learning how to express them healthily is a true superpower. It's time to break free from the stereotype and discover the strength in acknowledging and understanding your feelings.

Think of your emotions as waves in the ocean of life. Each wave is unique - anger, joy, sadness, excitement - they all have their own rhythm. Recognizing these waves is crucial for your mental well-being.

It allows you to respond appropriately in different situations, fostering better relationships and empowering you to make wise decisions.

Instead of suppressing or acting out impulsively, here's a powerful strategy: Pause & Reflect. Take a deep breath and ride out the storm until the waves become manageable. Then, dive deep into the source of your emotion. What triggered it?

Understanding the cause gives you the power to express yourself appropriately.

Here's a simple four-step process to express your emotions healthily: **Identify** the emotion, **understand** its source, **decide** how to express it, and **communicate assertively** and **respectfully**.

Real-Life Story: Jordan and Alex

Borrowing without asking... it's a little thing, isn't it?

But sometimes, it's the small stings that sting the most. Take for instance Jordan and Alex, two best friends who shared everything - laughter, secrets, even video games.

One day, Jordan discovered his favorite video game was missing from his collection. After some sleuthing around, he found out that Alex had taken it without permission - a surprise that stirred a whirlwind of emotions in him.

At first, Jordan felt an intense rush of anger. His face reddened and his heart pounded like a drum in his chest. It was clear: he needed to respond to this situation constructively rather than let these feelings fester.

So he took a deep breath and started with step one: **identifying** his emotion.

He asked himself what exactly he was feeling - anger or something else. After some introspection, he realized disappointment lurked beneath the red-hot surface of anger; disappointment in Alex for overstepping boundaries.

Next, came **understanding** its source – why did this action elicit such strong feelings?

Was it about just a video game? Or something deeper? An article published in the Journal of Personality and Social Psychology suggests we often react strongly when our trust is violated because it goes against our expectations of fairness.

That's when Jordan understood; **it wasn't about the game but about trust** – Alex taking something without asking had breached their mutual trust.

Now knowing the root cause, Jordan took the third step and **decided** to express these emotions healthily instead of lashing out impulsively.

He chose non-aggressive communication - expressing feelings **assertively** but **respectfully** with Alex. Instead of accusing him directly or letting pent-up frustration dictate their conversation's tone, Jordan approached him calmly yet firmly.

"Alex," he said earnestly "When I noticed you'd borrowed my video game without asking me first...it hurt." He paused then continued "I value trust between us more than anything else."

By following these steps – identifying his emotion as disappointment rather than raw anger, tracing its source back to violated trust not merely a lost game item; deciding on a healthy mode of expression through non-aggressive communication; and finally conveying those emotions assertively yet respectfully – Jordan made sure both parties' respect remained intact while successfully addressing an issue that could've been swept under the rug otherwise.

The same principles can apply whenever we encounter situations where we need to express our emotions healthily – recognizing them accurately for what they are rather than letting them become distorted or magnified beyond proportion.

So, my fellow emotions explorers, let's break free from the stereotypes, embrace our feelings, and show the world that being in touch with our emotions is a strength, not a weakness. It's time to unleash the power of emotional intelligence and ride the waves of life with confidence and courage!

Ah-ha Moment: Here's the ultimate realization - understanding your own emotions not only helps you navigate your own life but also fosters empathy toward others. By acknowledging that everyone experiences these waves in their own way, you can build deeper connections and become a superhero of emotions.

Building Empathy Toward Others

Let's start by defining empathy; it is not feeling bad for someone else; rather, it's about seeing things from their viewpoint. Think about stepping into their shoes and walking around in them for a day or two.

We all have our own unique perspectives, shaped by our experiences and backgrounds. But what if we could step into someone else's shoes and truly understand their world? That's where empathy comes in, my friend. It's like a superpower that allows us to connect with others on a deeper level.

Empathy isn't just feeling sorry for someone; it's about truly *seeing and understanding their emotions and experiences and trying to feel what they are feeling.*

Imagine you're playing Call Of Duty and you are locked in the middle of an intense battle when suddenly your Wi-Fi crashes. Frustrating, right?

Now consider how much more frustrating it must be for those who don't even have access to decent Wi-Fi or gaming consoles in the first place! That's empathy - putting yourself in their shoes and understanding their struggles.

So why should we care about empathy? Well, for starters, it makes us more human. It strengthens our relationships, resolves conflicts, and brings more happiness into our lives. Plus, studies have shown that *empathetic individuals tend to have better overall well-being.*

So let's get down to business – How can we build empathy?

1) **Listen Actively**: This means not only hearing words but also grasping the emotions behind them. Next time when a friend shares his problems try focusing less on advice-giving and more on just listening actively.

2) **Practice Perspective-Taking**: This involves imagining how others feel about certain situations. For instance, if your friend didn't invite you over for his birthday party instead of getting angry think about possible reasons like maybe he was having family issues or financial constraints.

3) **Engage with Diverse Groups**: Try talking to people outside your immediate circle- different age groups, cultures etcetera; this broadens horizons and enhances understanding of varied experiences.

4) **Reflect On Your Own Experiences**: Remember times when you felt similar emotions as others are expressing now – this helps relate better with their situation.

What if building empathy seems tough? Don't worry! Like any new skill being mastered (like perfecting headshots in COD), developing empathy requires time too!

Keep practicing small steps every day until they become second nature to you! But always remember, while you're busy understanding and caring for others, take care of yourself too. You need to be emotionally strong to support others effectively.

And don't let anyone tell you that empathy is a weakness. It's a superpower that sets you apart and earns the respect of your peers and adults alike.

Developing Self-Esteem and Confidence

Self-esteem is like a beacon that lights up our lives, giving us the confidence and strength to conquer any challenge that comes our way. It illuminates our path, empowering us to navigate through life's winding roads with confidence and determination; it's like a sturdy ship that can weather any storm. However, building self-esteem isn't as easy as snapping together a Lego set. It requires some work, my friend.

When we talk about self-esteem, we're talking about how much we **value ourselves**. It's like being the primary shareholder in an internal stock market. Are your stocks rising or falling? The answer to this question affects how we navigate the world.

Think of yourself as a unique genius, just like Albert Einstein said. Embrace all your strengths and abilities, and *don't judge yourself by someone else's standards*. You're a beautiful mosaic made up of different pieces.

Now, let's dive into some practical steps for boosting your self-esteem:

1. **Love Yourself**: Embrace all of who you are—the good, the bad, and the ugly. You're a masterpiece, my friend and you are 100% unique.

2. **Positive Vibes**: Feed your mind with positive thoughts and affirmations. It's like giving your brain a daily dose of sunlight. A daily dose of uplifting

affirmations can work wonders in boosting self-esteem.

3. **Small Wins**: Set some small achievable goals. Maybe you'll conquer a one mile bike ride today. Every victory counts!

4. **No Comparison**: Apples and oranges are both delicious, but they're different. Don't compare yourself to others. You're unique in your own way.

Now, let's talk about the enemy: ***negative self-talk.*** It's like poison for our self-esteem, but we have a powerful antidote—positive affirmations!

They act like white knights battling against these dark thoughts inside our heads. Something as simple as looking at yourself in the mirror each morning and saying out loud three times 'I am smart, I am handsome, I am amazing' will boost your self-esteem greatly.

"Emotional intelligence is the compass that guides us through the intricate landscape of human interactions, fostering understanding, connection, and personal growth." Unknown

But what if your self-esteem feels like rock bottom?

When it feels like you're walking on burning coals? In those moments, seeking professional help isn't a weakness; it's a sign of strength and courage and I strongly recommend you reach out to someone who can help you.

Ah-ha Moment: Your worth doesn't come from external people or things. It comes from within you. Seeking approval from others or chasing material possessions won't bring lasting happiness. It's about valuing yourself and investing in your own growth and development.

Building self-esteem is like constructing a fortress. It takes time and effort, but with each brick you lay, your foundation grows stronger. So, start building your fortress today and create a sanctuary filled with unwavering self-esteem. You deserve it!

Handling Rejection and Failure Gracefully

Dealing with rejection may seem like getting hit by an icy blast, but here's the exciting part - it's not the end of the world!

Just like a skilled blacksmith shapes iron into incredible art, we too can use rejection as a tool to forge ourselves into stronger individuals.

Think of life as a grand adventure, sailing through an ocean of opportunities. Along the way, you'll encounter islands of yes's and no's. Our job is to navigate these waters without letting the waves of rejection sink our spirits.

Here's the secret: Embrace rejection as a chance to learn and grow. Science tells us that our brains process rejection in a *similar way to physical pain*. So, instead of brushing off those feelings, acknowledge them. Treat each "no" as a stepping stone towards self-improvement.

Real-Life Story: Walt Disney

Take a page from the resilience playbook of some of the best know people in the world. J.K. Rowling faced rejection from multiple publishers before finding success with Harry Potter. And don't forget Walt Disney, who was told he lacked imagination before creating an empire of magic that expands around the whole world! They didn't let rejection define them; they used it as fuel to keep pushing forward.

Now, let's dive into the tactics.

Change your perspective on rejection. See it as *feedback* rather than failure. When faced with a "no," ask yourself what you did well and how you can improve. Turn negative emotions into constructive criticism that fuels your future growth.

And remember, patience is a virtue. Just like a gardener waits for seeds to blossom, give yourself time to develop and nurture your skills. Good things take time so keep persisting, knocking on doors, and seeking new opportunities.

So, my fellow adventurer, let rejection be your path to success. Embrace the no's, learn from them, and keep moving forward. Because in the end, rejection isn't a reflection of your worth; it's just a part of the incredible journey we call life.

Key Takeaways

- Use the four-step process to *Identify* the emotion, *understand* its source, *decide* how to express it, and *communicate assertively* and *respectfully.*

- Emotional openness isn't common among teenagers but striving towards it yields healthier outcomes.

- Being empathetic fosters stronger relationships & resolves conflicts.

- Building empathy requires active listening skills & engaging diverse groups among other methods.

- Feed your mind with positive affirmations to build your self-esteem.

- Seeking professional help isn't a weakness; it's a sign of strength and courage.

- Each rejection is not failure but feedback aimed at refining performance.

- Build resilience by developing patience and persistence.

Chapter 5: Resolving Conflict

In the exhilarating adventure of adolescence, conflicts often arise like unexpected hurdles on the path to self-discovery and manhood. As a developing boy, you are no stranger to these confrontations, be it with family members, friends, or even facing the troubling specter of bullying.

But fear not! This chapter is your guide to resolving conflict with grace and confidence, empowering you to overcome obstacles and foster healthier relationships.

Together, we will explore three key aspects: navigating conflict at home, addressing disagreements among friends, and understanding what bullying is and how to stand up against it.

Navigating Conflict at Home

Home is where the heart is, they say, but it's also where clashes and disagreements can sometimes feel most intense. Whether it's a difference in opinions, competing interests (like you want to watch different Foxtel channels), or simply the daily pressures of living under one roof, conflict within the family is an inevitable part of life.

As a tween or teen, learning how to navigate these conflicts can help foster healthier relationships with your parents and siblings, and contribute to a more harmonious home environment.

First and foremost, it's important to recognize that conflict is a *normal part of family dynamics*. Each family member brings their own unique perspectives, experiences, and expectations, which can lead to clashes in beliefs, values, and desires.

It's essential to understand that disagreements don't necessarily indicate a lack of love or respect within the family. Instead, they present opportunities for growth, understanding, and finding common ground.

When faced with conflict at home, one key approach is effective communication. Expressing your thoughts, feelings, and concerns in a calm and respectful manner can help open up lines of dialogue and foster a deeper understanding among family members.

It's important to actively listen to others, allowing them to share their perspectives *without* interruption or judgment. Through active listening, you can gain insights into their experiences and feelings, promoting empathy and mutual understanding.

In addition to communication, another crucial aspect of resolving conflict at home is compromise and finding win-

win solutions. It's natural for family members to have differing needs and desires, but finding a middle ground or alternative that satisfies everyone involved can lead to more satisfying resolutions.

This requires a willingness to be flexible, considerate, and open-minded, as well as a recognition that everyone's opinions and feelings are valid.

Ah-ha Moment: Remember, compromise doesn't mean giving up on what's important to you but rather finding ways to meet each other halfway.

Furthermore, conflict within the family can often stem from unmet expectations or misunderstandings. Taking the time to reflect on your own expectations and communicating them clearly can help avoid unnecessary conflicts.

Similarly, seeking to understand the expectations of others and finding common ground can foster a greater sense of unity and cooperation. It's important to approach these discussions with empathy and respect, acknowledging that everyone's needs and perspectives are valuable.

Addressing Disagreements Among Friends

Friendships are an integral part of adolescence, offering companionship, support, and shared experiences.

However, even the closest of friendships can encounter disagreements and conflicts. Learning how to address these issues in a respectful and constructive manner can strengthen your bonds with friends and contribute to a more positive social environment.

When facing disagreements among friends, one important aspect is active listening. Give your friends the space to express their thoughts and feelings without interruption and show genuine interest in understanding their perspectives.

This helps foster empathy and demonstrates that you value their opinions and emotions. Avoid making assumptions or jumping to conclusions, as this can lead to misunderstandings and further conflict. Instead, ask clarifying questions to ensure a clear understanding of their point of view.

Open and honest communication is vital in resolving conflicts with friends. Clearly express your thoughts, feelings, and concerns, using "I" statements to avoid sounding accusatory. Share how certain actions or situations have made you feel and be specific about what behavior or issue you would like to address. It's important to maintain a calm and non-confrontational tone, allowing for constructive dialogue rather than a heated argument. Remember, the goal is to find a resolution that satisfies both parties and strengthens the friendship.

> *"Conflict cannot survive without your participation." - Wayne Dyer*

Another key aspect in resolving conflicts among friends is the willingness to compromise. Friendships involve give-and-take, and finding a middle ground can help maintain a balanced and mutually satisfying relationship.

Consider the perspectives and needs of your friends and be open to finding solutions that accommodate everyone involved. This requires flexibility, empathy, and a focus on maintaining the connection and well-being of the friendship.

Real-Life Example: Tanner, Max and Ethan

Meet Tanner, a high school junior known for his easy-going nature and constant smile. His circle of friends was as diverse as can be - from Max, the math whiz, to Ethan, the drama king, they were a rainbow of personalities.

But one day, things took an unexpected turn. Max needed support for a prestigious mathematics competition, while Ethan was gearing up for the lead role in the school play. The tension grew thick as both boys pushed their agendas, and Tanner found himself caught in the crossfire.

Imagine being in Tanner's shoes - torn between your closest friends and their dreams. It's tough, right? But Tanner remembered something important - the power of science. According to Dr. Susan Heitler's study on conflict resolution, collaborative problem solving is the key.

So, our smart friend Tanner decided to openly acknowledge both Max's ambition and Ethan's passion *without favoring one over the other.* He proposed a solution that divided his time amongst both his friends, ensuring equal support for both.

And guess what? It worked like magic! The boys realized that their rivalry was petty compared to the value of their friendship. Max secured second place in the math competition, and Ethan received standing ovations for his performance.

In the end, Tanner showed us that empathy and rational thinking can resolve even the most heated disagreements among friends.

So, remember this valuable lesson - when faced with clashing opinions, let your heart be guided by reason and understanding. Just like Tanner, you'll find that it works wonders every time!

Bullying – What it is and How to Stand Up Against It

Bullying is an unfortunate reality that many teenagers face, and it can have a profound impact on one's emotional well-being and self-esteem. Understanding what bullying entails and learning how to stand up against it is crucial for creating a safe and inclusive environment for all.

Bullying can take various forms, including physical, verbal, or cyberbullying. It involves repeated aggressive behavior intended to harm, intimidate, or exert power over another person.

It's important to recognize that bullying is never acceptable and should never be tolerated. If you witness or experience bullying, it's essential to take action to address the situation and support those affected.

Standing up against bullying requires courage, empathy, and assertiveness. If you witness someone being bullied, be an ally by speaking up and intervening in a safe manner. Offer support to the victim and encourage them to seek help from trusted adults or authorities. Avoid participating in or condoning bullying behaviors, as this only perpetuates the cycle of harm.

It's crucial to foster a culture of respect, empathy, and inclusivity among your peers. Treat others with kindness and acceptance, and actively challenge harmful stereotypes or prejudices. Stand up for those who may be targeted or marginalized and promote a sense of unity and understanding.

Remember, by standing together against bullying, you create a safer and more supportive environment for everyone.

Key Takeaways

- Use 'I' statements instead of 'You' accusations to express yourself better during conflicts.

- Understand that it's okay not to agree on everything. Everybody is allowed to have their own opinion.

- Find common ground. Despite differences, there may be aspects both parties agree upon.

- Give each other space If needed. Sometimes stepping back helps clear minds aiding rational decision-making later on.

Chapter 6: Dealing with Stress and Anxiety

You're at a stage in life where you are no longer a child but not yet an adult. It's the brink of a thrilling new chapter in life, where challenges and pressures may seem overwhelming.

But fear not, my friend! This chapter is here to guide you through the unique stressors of your teenage years and empower you with the tools to navigate them with resilience and understanding.

As a teenager, you're in the midst of a whirlwind of change – physically, emotionally, socially, and academically. It's like juggling a thousand things at once while trying to figure out who you are and where you fit in this vast world. It's no wonder that stress can creep in and affect your mental health and overall well-being.

But let's unravel the mystery of stress. It's a natural part of life, our response to challenges and threats. However, chronic stress can take a toll on both your body and mind, leading to anxiety, depression, and even physical ailments. That's why it's crucial for you to learn how to manage stress effectively and avoid it becoming a constant burden.

Studies have shown that a staggering 56% of students experience extreme stress during the school year, often fueled by overwhelming homework (Pope et al., 2013). This pressure can push you towards unhealthy coping mechanisms like overeating or sleep deprivation, which only worsen the stress levels.

Now, let's talk about Chris, your neighbor who poured his heart and soul into basketball but missed making it to the state team. The disappointment hit him hard, and it lingered for weeks, affecting not only his emotional well-being but also his academic performance. But here's a reminder for you, my friend: ***it's okay to not have everything figured out right now.***

"In the journey of life, uncertainties are part of the adventure." - Unknown

This quote reminds us that it's normal to feel unsure or anxious about the future, especially during this phase of life. Instead of suppressing these feelings, embrace them, knowing that they are small bumps on the way to discovering your true path and aspirations.

Through my own experiences, I've discovered that practical solutions are often more effective than abstract stress-management techniques. For example, let's say you are a perfectionist overwhelmed by the pressure of grades. By developing healthy study habits, such as taking breaks and setting realistic goals, you will be able to significantly reduce anxiety and boost confidence in managing academic demands.

Let's explore some of the stressors commonly experienced during the teen years:

- Peer pressure can be intense and influence decision-making. The desire for independence clashes with parental expectations.

- Body image issues arise due to societal standards and comparisons.

- Online bullying has emerged as a significant threat to mental health.

So, my friend, as you embark on this journey through adolescence, remember that while stress is inevitable, your mindset and approach can make all the difference.

Growing up is a challenging process, but within those challenges lie incredible opportunities for personal development and growth. Embrace the adventure, my friend, and enjoy the ride towards becoming the person you truly want to be!"

Coping Mechanisms for Stress Relief

We know all too well that life can sometimes feel like a wild roller coaster ride, where stress sneaks up on us like a thrill-seeking passenger who forgot to fasten their seatbelt.

But fear not, because in this section, we're going to equip you with the tools you need to conquer stress like a true champ.

> *"Life is like a roller coaster, my dude.*
> *Embrace it, enjoy the ride, and live it to the*
> *fullest." - Avril Lavigne*

First things first, let's decode what stress really is. Think of it as your body's way of waving a red flag, signaling that something needs your attention.

Just like ignoring car troubles can lead to a breakdown, ignoring your body's stress signals can have serious consequences for your mental and physical well-being down the line.

So, how do we tackle stress head-on? Buckle up, and get ready for these powerful coping mechanisms:

1. Take a Breather

Yes, you read that right dude. When stress hits hard, our breathing becomes shallow and fast, sending us spiraling into a state of anxiety. The antidote? Deep belly breathing exercises. Trust me, they work like magic to instantly calm your racing heart and help you find your zen.

Here's a simple belly breathing exercise you can practice anytime, anywhere:

- ✓ Find a comfortable position: Sit or lie down in a comfortable position, making sure your back is straight but relaxed. You can close your eyes if it helps you focus.

- ✓ Place your hands on your belly: Gently place one hand on your chest and the other hand on your belly, right below your ribcage.

- ✓ Take a deep breath in: Slowly inhale through your nose, letting your belly rise as you fill your lungs with air. Feel your hand on your belly move outward as it expands.

- ✓ Exhale slowly: Gradually exhale through your mouth, allowing your belly to deflate and your hand to lower. Focus on releasing all the air from your lungs.

- ✓ Repeat and relax: Continue this pattern of deep belly breathing, inhaling through your nose and exhaling through your mouth. Take your time with each breath and try to make each one slower and deeper than the last.

2. Sweat It Out

Ever heard of the runner's high? It's a burst of happiness triggered by those amazing endorphins released during exercise – the "feel-good hormones" that give stress a serious beatdown. So grab your sneakers, hit the court, the trails, or the gym, and let those endorphins work their magic!

Even just a 15 – 30 min burst of exercise will make you feel a whole lot happier, so put on your joggers and get out there!

3. Unplug and Unwind

In this digital age, being constantly connected can add unnecessary stress to our already overflowing plates. That's why regular "digital detoxes" are essential.

Disconnect from the virtual world and reconnect with yourself, my friend. Your mind and soul will thank you for it.

4. Fuel Up Right

You wouldn't pour soda into a high-performance sports machine, right? Well, think of your body as a top-notch sports car. Treat it with respect by nourishing it with wholesome, nutritious food.

Trust me, the right fuel will keep your brain firing on all cylinders, helping you tackle daily pressures with ease.

4. Embrace the Power of Zzz's

Sleep, my dude, is the secret weapon against stress. While you snooze, your brain processes the day's events and emotions, ensuring your emotional well-being stays in top shape. So, prioritize good quality sleep like a boss, and wake up ready to conquer the world!

Ah-ha Moment: Stress isn't always the bad guy – in small doses, it can motivate us. But when it becomes overwhelming, it's time to bust out the stress-relief techniques!

Now, here's a pro tip: Don't fall for those quick-fix promises. We're all unique individuals, so coping strategies will vary from person to person. There's no one-size-fits-all solution, but by understanding what triggers your stress and implementing these kick-ass coping mechanisms, you'll gain the upper hand and conquer stress like a true warrior.

And hey, if things ever get too overwhelming, never hesitate to reach out for help. School counselors and mental health professionals are there for a reason – they've got the tools to tackle even the toughest challenges.

Remember, stress is a universal experience. It's how we manage it that sets us apart. So gear up, embrace the ride, and let's master the art of stress relief together, paving the way for happier, healthier lives!

Seeking Help When Needed

When life throws you a curveball and you're stuck in a tough spot, it's easy to freeze up like a deer caught in headlights.

In those moments, it might feel like asking for help is admitting defeat. But let me tell you something my young friend – seeking help is not a sign of weakness. *It takes true courage and strength to reach out and ask for assistance when you need it most.*

Our society often values independence and self-sufficiency, and while those traits are important, they should never stop us from seeking support. Having the humility to recognize our limitations and ask for guidance shows a level of maturity that goes far beyond relying solely on ourselves.

Now, let's dive deep into this topic. It's common for teenagers, especially us guys, to shy away from seeking help because we fear *judgment* or *embarrassment*. We think that doing everything on our own makes us more grown-up, but let me tell you something – even adults need help sometimes!

Real-Life Story: Meet James

James was struggling with his math homework but was too afraid to ask his teacher for extra help because he didn't want to appear stupid in front of his classmates. So he resorted to late-night study sessions, trying to decipher those complex equations on his own, which only led to frustration and exhaustion.

Finally, he reached a breaking point and swallowed his pride, approaching his teacher after class one day to explain his struggles honestly. To his surprise, instead of mocking him, his teacher showed understanding and patience. They dedicated extra time each week to help James catch up, and eventually, math became one of his strongest subjects!

Remember the words of Albert Einstein, who said, "The more I learn, the more I realize how much I don't know." This quote perfectly captures why it's crucial to seek knowledge not just independently but also through the wisdom of others around us.

So, how do we overcome the hesitation that comes with seeking help?

First, remind yourself that ***everyone needs assistance at some point*** – we're all human!

Second, shift your mindset to focus on growth and learning rather than seeing requests for help as signs of weakness or incompetence.

There's plenty of research out there that shows the power of collaboration and community. Studies have found that individuals participating in group-based weight loss programs, for example, were significantly more likely to achieve their desired results compared to those who tried to lose weight alone.

We can apply these insights to various aspects of life, whether it's academics, sports, or personal relationships.

- ✓ If you're stuck on a homework assignment, reach out to your classmates or teachers for a clearer explanation.

- ✓ Struggling to master a new move at football practice? Don't hesitate to ask your coach for tips and techniques to improve.

- ✓ Feeling overwhelmed by anxiety or depression? Talk to someone you trust, whether it's a therapist, counselor, or a supportive friend.

Recognize that managing your emotions is an integral part of growing up.

According to the American Psychological Association, the majority of teens report significant levels of stress, yet nearly half of them say they do nothing to manage it. Let that sink in for a moment – *that's an alarming statistic, isn't it?*

So, my friend, the next time you find yourself struggling, take action. Recognize that it's okay to need help, identify someone you can turn to for relevant advice, articulate your issue as clearly as possible, and be open to receiving feedback without taking it personally.

Remember, the journey of growth and development is a constant process of learning and unlearning, and a key component of that is the willingness to learn from others. So, the next time you hesitate to ask a question, remember that it's a brave and wise decision to make.

Key Takeaways

- Stress is normal, but chronic stress needs management.

- It's important to recognize signs of excessive chronic stress and seek professional help when needed.

- Master the art of deep belly breathing exercises.

- Prioritize good quality sleep like a boss.

- Recognize that managing emotions is an integral part growing up; ignoring them only exacerbates problem!

- There no shame admitting we don't have all answers; there's always something learn others.

- Don't hesitate to seek help when stress becomes overwhelming.

- Recognize your limits, set realistic goals.

Chapter 7: Understanding Diversity and Inclusion

Understanding diversity and inclusion is crucial as you navigate through your teenage years. It means recognizing and embracing the unique qualities that make each person special, whether it's their culture, race, sexual orientation, or gender identity.

When we value diversity, we create a world where everyone feels accepted and respected for who they are.

Diversity is about more than just differences in appearance; it's about the beautiful variety of experiences, ideas, and perspectives that exist in our global community. By understanding and appreciating diversity, you expand your own horizons and gain a deeper understanding of the world. It opens your mind to different ways of thinking, challenges your assumptions, and helps you grow into a well-rounded individual.

Inclusion goes hand in hand with diversity. It's about ensuring that everyone has a seat at the table and that their voices are heard. Inclusive spaces embrace people from all walks of life, creating an environment where everyone feels valued and empowered. When you actively promote inclusion, you foster a sense of belonging and harmony, celebrating the uniqueness of each individual and building stronger, more compassionate communities.

So, as you journey through your teenage years, remember the importance of understanding diversity and practicing inclusion. Embrace the differences that make our world rich and vibrant. Stand up against discrimination, challenge stereotypes, and create spaces where everyone feels safe, respected, and free to express their true selves.

Together, we can create a world that celebrates the beauty of diversity and ensures that no one is left behind. Understanding diversity and inclusion is crucial for building a kickass society where everyone feels respected and accepted.

Respect for all Cultures and Races

Respecting all cultures and races means recognizing the awesomeness that comes with different traditions, customs, and histories. Each culture brings unique knowledge and perspectives to the table, so it's like a treasure trove of coolness.

It's not just about different skin tones or languages; it's a mind-blowing tapestry of perspectives, histories, and experiences that shape our human story. As you grow into a young adult in today's global society, one of the most crucial skills you can develop is respect for all cultures and races.

So, what does respect really mean when it comes to cultures and races? It's not about blindly agreeing with every practice or tradition you come across. It's about recognizing their significance within their cultural context.

When we make an effort to understand and appreciate diverse cultures, we break down barriers and build bridges of understanding, bringing people together in unity and cooperation.

Now, let's dive into some practical ways you can cultivate this respect.

- ✓ First, educate yourself. Read books by authors from different corners of the globe, watch documentaries that showcase diverse societies, and check out international news outlets to get varied perspectives on global events. And remember, education doesn't always happen in a classroom – casual conversations can be just as enlightening!

- ✓ Secondly, embrace opportunities to interact directly with people from other cultures. These interactions will give you firsthand insights that go beyond what any book or documentary can offer. Research shows that exposure to multicultural environments boosts empathy towards different racial groups and reduces prejudice. It's all about breaking down those walls and building bridges of understanding.

Fear lies at the heart of racism and cultural intolerance – fear of what's different or unknown. Overcoming this fear takes conscious effort to better understand those differences, fostering mutual respect among various racial groups.

"Strength lies in differences, not in similarities" Stephen Covey

In the fight against racism and cultural intolerance, let's keep in mind that understanding breeds acceptance. Strive always to learn before forming judgments. Celebrate the unique traditions of every culture, like Japan's cherry blossom viewing parties or the vibrant festivals of India.

And remember, language barriers often lead to misunderstandings, so try learning a few phrases when interacting with someone from another culture. It goes a long way in building connections.

Acceptance of Different Sexual Orientations, Embracing the Rainbow Spectrum

Just as every color in the rainbow shines with its own vibrant hue, every individual on this planet possesses their own distinct identity. And one essential aspect of this identity is sexual orientation—a core part of who you are and how you connect with others.

Accepting different sexual orientations and gender identities is key to creating a world where everyone can be themselves without fear of being judged or treated differently. We need to celebrate love in all its forms and recognize that identity *isn't just a one-size-fits-all thing.*

To understand sexual orientation better, let's dive into some science. Studies reveal that sexual orientation isn't a choice or something that can be changed; it's as innate as your eye color or whether you're left-handed or right-handed (Balthazart, J. 2020).

Think about it for a moment—did you ever decide to be attracted to girls? Or was it just something natural, like having brown or blonde hair? The same applies to other people's sexual orientations too — they don't choose whom they're attracted to any more than you do.

Scientists have proposed various theories about what shapes our sexual orientation—biological factors like genetics and hormones, environmental influences, or a combination of both. But regardless of how someone identifies—straight, gay, bisexual, queer—what truly matters is respecting the rights and dignity of all human beings.

You've probably heard the saying, "variety is the spice of life." Well, that holds true when it comes to human sexuality too! Imagine a world where everyone only loved vanilla ice cream—it would be pretty dull and monotonous!

It can sometimes feel confusing — this whole realm of different sexual orientations — especially if it goes against societal norms or clashes with personal or religious beliefs. It's okay to feel confused because confusion often leads us to understand.

Ah-ha Moment: Acceptance doesn't mean agreement — it means acknowledging another person's right to live authentically without discrimination, regardless of differing viewpoints on sexuality.

Your best friend might come out as gay tomorrow — or maybe they already have — and they still deserve your love and friendship just as before, because their essence hasn't changed; they have simply shared another layer of their complex self with you. They are still the same person that you enjoy hanging out with.

What truly matters is not if someone is straight or gay—simply if that person is kind-hearted and genuine.

So here's your challenge: if somebody opens up about their sexuality, listen without judgment and respond with empathy, because their courage deserves nothing less. And remember, if there comes a day when you question your own sexuality, be gentle with yourself too.

If these emotions become overwhelming, seek help from trusted adults around you—perhaps a teacher? Or turn to professional organizations specifically designed to support young people grappling with questions regarding sexuality, like 'The Trevor Project' or 'GLSEN' – the Gay Lesbian and Straight Education Network.

Now, let's prepare for an extra-bad scenario: what if bullying occurs based on someone's sexual preference? In that case, if it's safe to do so, intervene directly by standing beside them, showing solidarity. Report it, and you could potentially save lives.

Remember, the world needs more heroes willing to stand up against injustice, not bystanders idly watching from the sidelines filming it for Tik Tok.

Gender Equality – Challenging Stereotypes

And let's not forget about gender equality. It's all about treating everyone equally, regardless of their gender. We need to break down those outdated stereotypes and make sure everyone has the same opportunities and rights.

When we champion gender equality, we're creating a world where all genders can kick butt and make a difference.

In our society, there are certain expectations placed on boys and girls. Boys are often told to be strong, tough, and emotionless, while girls are expected to be soft, nurturing, and emotional.

These stereotypes have influenced our behavior and created unfair expectations. It's time for us to challenge these stereotypes and redefine what it truly means to be a man.

Think of stereotypes as shortcuts that our brains use to understand complex social situations. They're like expressways that quickly get us from one point to another, but they often overlook the diverse experiences and perspectives along the way.

What if we told you that being strong is not just about physical strength, but also about standing up against injustice? What if being tough means having the courage to express your emotions openly and honestly?

Let's break free from the limitations of stereotypical masculinity. Embrace your emotions and understand that they don't make you weak; *they make you human.* It's okay to feel sad, and it's okay to cry. In fact, expressing your emotions openly takes incredible strength and defies societal expectations.

It's also important to recognize and promote equality across genders. Treat everyone with respect and fairness, not just because it's the right thing to do, but because it's a fundamental human right.

Remember, promoting equality is not just about women's rights; it's about recognizing and valuing the rights of all individuals, regardless of their gender.

Don't be afraid to engage in tasks that are traditionally considered feminine. Cooking dinner or doing laundry doesn't diminish your masculinity. Embrace these tasks as opportunities to challenge gender norms and expand your skills. Would you say Gordon Ramsay was not masculine? I doubt it.

Let's challenge the stereotypes, express our emotions, treat everyone equally, and break free from the limitations of traditional masculinity. It won't be easy, but the rewards at the end are worth every effort.

This journey towards breaking gender stereotypes requires patience, resilience & bravery—but trust us when we say—the rewards at the end are worth every effort!

Becoming an Ally – How to Support Others

You may have encountered the term "ally" in today's interconnected world, but what does it mean?

Being an ally is more than just a label; it's about taking action, having the right attitude, and truly understanding the experiences of marginalized communities.

An ally is someone who supports and amplifies the voices of those in marginalized communities, using their own privilege to challenge inequality. Being an ally isn't always easy, but it's important for personal growth and making a positive impact.

So, how can you become an ally? It starts with education and learning about the experiences and challenges faced by people outside your own sphere of experience.

Empathy plays a crucial role in being an ally and putting yourself in someone else's shoes through perspective-taking exercises can foster understanding and compassion.

To become a better ally, educate yourself about different cultures, listen actively to diverse perspectives, and take action against unfair treatment whenever you witness it. Small changes can have a big impact, and your efforts as an ally can make a difference in the lives of those around you.

Real-Life example: Robert and Sophia

Let's consider the case of Robert, a high school student who exemplified allyship in a real-life situation.

During cultural awareness week at school, Robert noticed that his classmate, Sophia, was being targeted and ridiculed for wearing traditional clothing that represented her cultural heritage. Instead of remaining a bystander, Robert chose to take a stand and support Sophia.

Robert not only confronted the bullies but also went a step further. He realized the importance of understanding and appreciating Sophia's culture. So, he reached out to Sophia after the incident, expressing his genuine interest in learning more about her traditions and the significance of her clothing.

Through conversations and research, Robert actively educated himself about her cultural heritage, showing respect and curiosity. By standing up for Sophia and actively seeking to understand her background, Robert not only validated her experience but also fostered an environment of inclusivity and acceptance.

His actions had a positive impact, not just on Sophia but potentially on others who witnessed his genuine allyship. Robert's example reminds us that being an ally involves not only defending others but also actively engaging, learning, and embracing the diverse cultures that exist within our community.

Key Takeaways

- Respect for all cultures and races begins with open-mindedness - a willingness to listen without judgment.

- Sexual orientation isn't a choice—it's inherent.

- Respond with empathy when someone confides in you about their sexuality.

- Seek help if you feel overwhelmed by emotions related to your own or others' sexual preferences.

- Don't shy away from traditionally feminine tasks.

Conclusion

Congratulations! You've completed a transformative journey through the pages of "Navigating Adolescence: Essential Life Skills Every Boy Needs to Know."

As you close this chapter, you're equipped with an array of essential life skills that will empower you to face the challenges and embrace the wonders of adolescence and beyond.

Throughout this book, we've delved into a diverse range of topics, each one crafted with the aim of helping you grow into a confident, well-rounded, and compassionate individual. From handling money wisely and becoming a kitchen whiz to building meaningful relationships and communicating effectively, you've gained valuable tools to create a fulfilling life.

By understanding consent, respecting boundaries, and nurturing emotional intelligence, you've laid the foundation for authentic connections with others and developed the resilience to navigate the ups and downs of life. You've also learned to resolve conflicts with grace and address the critical issue of bullying, ensuring you contribute to a kinder and more supportive community.

As we explored dealing with stress and anxiety, you've gained valuable insights into recognizing stressors and embracing healthy coping mechanisms. Remember, seeking help when needed is not a sign of weakness, but a sign of strength and self-awareness.

The final journey into understanding diversity and inclusion has expanded your perspective, fostering respect for all cultures, races, and sexual orientations. By challenging gender stereotypes, you've contributed to creating a more equal and accepting world.

As you venture forward, keep these life skills close to your heart. Embrace your individuality, for it is your uniqueness that makes you truly extraordinary. Continue to be open to learning, growing, and adapting as you navigate the ever-changing tides of life.

Always remember that mistakes are not failures; they are stepping stones toward growth. Embrace your journey with courage and resilience, and know that each experience, good or challenging, contributes to shaping the person you become.

Be kind to yourself and others, for empathy and understanding are powerful tools in fostering harmony and unity. As you interact with the world, let compassion guide your actions, and let respect be the cornerstone of your relationships.

Your adolescence is just the beginning of an incredible adventure. Embrace the challenges with a positive mindset and a thirst for knowledge, for within you lies the potential to create a future that is both extraordinary and meaningful.

Now, spread your wings, embark on new adventures, and face the world with the life skills you've acquired. As you navigate the vast ocean of life, always remember the wisdom you've gained here, and let it guide you toward a future filled with boundless possibilities.

Go forth and embrace every moment of your extraordinary journey. You've got this!

Before you go!

In exchange for all this, I've got just one more ask from you — kindly leave an honest review of how you found this book on Amazon.

Your comment will go a long way in convincing a brother going through a rough time to check out the message in this book.

References

Goddings AL, Mills KL, Clasen LS, Giedd JN, Viner RM, Blakemore SJ. The influence of puberty on subcortical brain development. Neuroimage. 2014 Mar;88:242-51. doi: 10.1016/j.neuroimage.2013.09.073. Epub 2013 Oct 11. PMID: 24121203; PMCID: PMC3991320.

https://pubmed.ncbi.nlm.nih.gov/24121203/

Marceau K, Dorn LD, Susman EJ. Stress and puberty-related hormone reactivity, negative emotionality, and parent-- adolescent relationships. Psychoneuroendocrinology. 2012 Aug;37(8):1286-98. doi: 10.1016/j.psyneuen.2012.01.001. Epub 2012 Jan 27. PMID: 22284540.

https://pubmed.ncbi.nlm.nih.gov/22284540/

Mortimer JT. The Benefits and Risks of Adolescent Employment. Prev Res. 2010 Jan 1;17(2):8-11.

https://www.researchgate.net/publication/46220880_The_Benefits_and_Risks_of_Adolescent_Employment

Charles Schwab Foundation's 'Teens & Money Survey' https://www.consumer-action.org/radar/articles/charles_schwab_foundations_teens_money_survey/

Attin T, Hornecker E. Tooth brushing and oral health: how frequently and when should tooth brushing be performed? Oral Health Prev Dent. 2005;3(3):135-40. PMID: 16355646.

https://pubmed.ncbi.nlm.nih.gov/16355646/

Centre for Disease Control. Show Me the Science – Why Wash Your Hands? 2023

https://www.cdc.gov/handwashing/why-handwashing.html

Weger, H., Bell, G., Minei, E., & Robinson, M. (2014). The Relative Effectiveness of Active Listening in Initial Interactions. International Journal of Listening, 28, 13 - 31.

https://doi.org/10.1080/10904018.2013.813234

Mehrabian Albert. Silent messages: implicit communication of emotions and attitudes. 2nd ed. Belmont, Calif., Wadsworth, 1981 (Originally published in 1971).

https://www.bl.uk/people/albert-mehrabian

Bámaca, M., & Umaña-Taylor, A. (2006). Testing a Model of Resistance to Peer Pressure Among Mexican-Origin Adolescents. Journal of Youth and Adolescence, 35, 626-640. https://doi.org/10.1007/S10964-006-9055-4.

Mollie Galloway, Jerusha Conner & Denise Pope (2013) Nonacademic Effects of Homework in Privileged, High-Performing High Schools, The Journal of Experimental Education, 81:4, 490-510.

https://www.tandfonline.com/doi/abs/10.1080/00220973.2012.745469

Balthazart, J. (2020). Sexual partner preference in animals and humans. Neuroscience & Biobehavioral Reviews, 115, 34-47.

https://doi.org/10.1016/j.neubiorev.2020.03.024

Coming Soon – Book #2

In the next installment, we're delving deeper into the world of possibilities, dreams, and personal growth, equipping you with essential life skills to thrive in an ever-changing world.

Setting Goals and Pursuing Passions: Discover your passions and interests and explore potential career paths that ignite your soul. Learn the art of setting SMART goals, propelling you forward with determination and focus. Embrace perseverance as you face obstacles on the road to your dreams, all while maintaining a balance between ambition and your own well-being.

Staying Safe Online: In the digital age, safeguarding your digital footprint and privacy is crucial. Gain the tools to recognize and combat cyberbullying, ensuring your online presence remains positive and responsible.

Maintaining Physical Health: A healthy body is the foundation of a fulfilling life. Learn the basics of nutrition and the significance of regular exercise in supporting your growing body. Gain valuable insights into understanding substance abuse risks and making responsible choices.

Giving Back to the Community: Discover the joy of giving back and the positive impact you can make both locally and globally. Find opportunities that align with your interests and values and uncover the true meaning of volunteerism.

Facing Adulthood: As you approach the threshold of adulthood, prepare for the next steps in your journey. Explore college or workforce options, learn about civic duty, and navigate the challenges of independence versus responsibility.

Join us once again on this empowering adventure, filled with wisdom, guidance, and inspiration.

As you venture into new territories, let "Navigating Adolescence - Part 2" be your trusted companion, supporting you as you blossom into the remarkable young man you were always destined to be. The world awaits, and the future is yours to create!

Printed in Great Britain
by Amazon

38136631R00066